Reviews & Comments

"...a valuable resource..."

This book is a valuable resource for any parent who asks the question *"How can I help my child become a lifelong reader?"* Jan Pierce's extensive background as a reading teacher gives her important insights into the processes necessary for a child to learn the complex skill known as reading. The book offers practical guidelines to encourage a child who may be struggling to read well.

Homegrown Reader: Simple Ways to Help Your Child Learn to Read is parent-friendly, giving specific examples that are easy to understand and implement at any stage of reading development. The message is clear: *"It's not just educators who teach a child to read. Parents can make a huge difference in developing a successful reader!"* The pathway to your child's reading success doesn't have to be a difficult one when you use the steps laid out in this informative book.

Cheryl Johnson, M.Ed.
Program Coordinator
Child Development Program
Washington State University, Vancouver

"...full of practical examples..."

Jan Pierce is a well-educated, experienced teacher with a passion for helping kids learn to love reading. Her book, ***Homegrown Readers: Simple Ways to Help Your Child Learn to Read*** is full of practical examples of ways parents can help their children both to learn to read and love to read. As a reading specialist and mom to three boys

I know the importance of parents taking an active roll in helping their children learn to read. In this book Jan Pierce outlines how to model reading to children, how to ask questions to promote comprehension, and how to engage your child in fun activities to extend understanding of a story. You will find this book a valuable resource as you help your child learn to read.

Heather Baron, M. Ed.
Reading Specialist
Evergreen School District
Vancouver, Washington

"Jan will help you learn, so you can help your children learn."

As a homeschool mother of eight children, I know the value of teaching children to read, and to read well. Parents of struggling learners and gifted ones will benefit from Jan's expertise as a reading specialist. She shares basic ideas, novel approaches to assist the reading process, thoughts on choosing good books to read, what to memorize and why, along with strategies good readers use. Just knowing what's important, and what is okay to let slide is a relief to many parents and their children.

Mrs. Pierce also gives us clues for choosing high interest books for our reluctant readers, along with keeping our children reading over the summer months. What is reading readiness? Jan will help you learn, so you can help your children learn. And she makes it fun and easy to do.

Kym Wright, Author, Writer
Owner of The Mother's Heart Magazine
Learn and Do Publications

"...she makes it fun and easy to do."

Homegrown Readers
Simple Ways To Help Your Child Learn To Read

Jan Pierce, M. Ed.

First Edition

Home Grown Readers:
Simple Ways to Help Your Child
Learn to Read
by Jan Pierce, M.Ed.

Printed in the United States of America

ISBN 978-0-9909764-0-0

Author's note regarding the use of gender terms:
Using 'he' or 'she' to determine gender can cause awkward sentence
structure. Whenever possible I've avoided the problem. Please know I am
speaking to both boys and girls and their reading needs throughout the text.

EDU029020 - EDUCATION, Teaching Methods & Materials, Reading
EDU017000 - EDUCATION, Home Schooling
EDU022000 - EDUCATION, Parent Participation

Table of Contents

Foreword

Parents This Book is for You..13

Chapter One

What is Reading Readiness?..15

Chapter Two

Cracking the Code: Why Learning to Read is
a Complex Process..25

Chapter Three

Bedtime Stories and More: Why It's So Important to
Read Aloud to Children..33

Chapter Four

Building Reading Skills: Why it's Okay to "Just Memorize".....43

Chapter Five

Strategies Good Readers Use..49

Chapter Six

Asking Questions to Improve Reading Comprehension..............59

Chapter Seven

Helping Children Choose a "Just Right" Book............67

Chapter Eight

Evaluating Your Child's Reading Skills............75

Chapter Nine

Retelling a Story: A Great Way to Measure Comprehension............83

Chapter Ten

Choosing High Interest Books for Reluctant Readers............89

Chapter Eleven

Ten Easy Ways to Make Reading More Fun............95

Chapter Twelve

Keep Them Reading Over the Summer
(and other school breaks)............103

Appendix I

Onsets, Rimes, Word Chunks and Word Families............113

Appendix II

Best Children's Author Websites............117

Appendix III

Best Reading Websites for Children............121

Appendix IV

Activities to Extend Reading Experiences....................127

Appendix V

Sample Story Maps and Other Graphic Organizers....................131

Appendix VI

Award Winning Books....................135

Appendix VII

Materials for Your Home Reading Center....................139

Appendix VIII

High Interest, Controlled Vocabulary Books
for Struggling Readers....................143

Appendix IX

Notes for Discussion Leaders....................153

Homegrown Readers Discussion Questions....................161

𝓗𝓸𝓶𝓮𝓰𝓻𝓸𝔀𝓷 𝓟𝓾𝓫𝓵𝓲𝓬𝓪𝓽𝓲𝓸𝓷𝓼
www.janpierce.net

Acknowledgements

*A very special thank you to the wonderful **Jan Brett**
for giving permission to use her books in our photo sessions.*

*Thanks to **Kym Wright** and the staff of **The Mother's Heart
Magazine** where the content of this book first appeared
as a series of articles.*

*Thanks to **Juliet Hambro**, entrepreneur and editor of
www.Askgranny.com for her vision, savvy and perseverance
in becoming the best.*

*Many Thanks to **Dr. Sue Stadler**, Reading Theory Specialist and
Instructional Coach, Evergreen Schools, Vancouver, WA for her
valuable advice and encouragement on this project.*

Dedications

For Roger, my best friend.
We're keeping the promise.

For my children, Josh and Kavita, Jon and Sara
– sources of love, laughter, purpose and joy.

For my grandsons Elijah, Jacob and Benjamin,
my favorite readers of all. You make me smile.

Foreword

Parents, this book is for you.

I began my teaching career in 1967 and retired in 2007. Over the course of my career I taught hundreds of children to read. It was my greatest joy, tracking the progress of first and second graders as they moved from careful and painstaking sounding to fluent reading.

There were always children who took to reading like a duck takes to water—they learned easily, quickly and enjoyed the process. Sadly, many others struggled every step of the way and remained challenged by the reading process. Although most children learned to use reading as a tool, some of them didn't learn to love it.

The reasons for difficulty in learning to read are many—it's a complicated process. But everyone can learn. My own children are a classic example of those who breeze through the process and those who must work harder to learn. My son knew his alphabet by the age of two and practically taught himself to read before kindergarten, in spite of a severe hearing loss. My daughter, who received the same exposure to books, struggled with the process and needed lots of extra practice to read fluently and comprehend well. She was an excellent student, however, and used strategies such as listening to tapes of assigned readings to help her gain meaning and save time.

If you're a parent, this book is for you. You want your children to learn to read. And whether they breeze through or hit a few bumps along the way, they will learn. This book will help you understand the learning to read process and encourage you to give the kinds of support that make reading both fun and effective. You're probably already reading aloud to your children and modeling a love of the written word. You're showing your children that reading is important.

As you read through the chapters, I hope you feel encouraged. It's never too late to gain new perspectives and learn a variety of ways to support your children as they solve reading challenges. Reading is the skill that opens the door to all other learning. We're wise to give it the attention it deserves and we can have fun along the way.

Remember, every child can improve reading skills. Some have to work harder. Together, we can do this.

Jan Pierce, M.Ed.

Feel free to contact me with your questions, problems or reports of great reading growth.

www.janpierce@comcast.net

www.janpierce.net

Chapter One

What is
Reading Readiness?

Chapter One

What is Reading Readiness?

I'm sitting on my living room couch with my three grandsons clustered around me—one on my lap and one on either side. We look a bit like a basket of puppies all wiggling and snuggling together. But we're doing more than just snuggling; we're reading. We're enjoying the rhythms and rhymes of a counting book, or the escapades of a naughty monkey, or the adventures of some children playing pirates. We're enjoying the world of books.

Did you notice I said *we're* reading? That's because all four of us are involved at the reading level just right for us. In truth only one of my grandsons is a fluent reader at age nine. The other two are in different stages of reading readiness. The youngest, just four, is nearly ready to understand the concept of letters making sounds and clusters of letters comprising words. The key word here is ready. He didn't arrive at this point of readiness by accident—he's been given countless "lessons" in reading from birth until today.

Before you start to worry that you'd have to be a certified teacher to provide your children that sort of reading readiness, let me put your mind at ease. Anyone can gift their children with reading readiness skills if they decide to do so. It's all about determining your home will provide an environment for learning and then doing it.

Your Home: A Learning Environment

Reading experts say a child should have heard at least five hundred stories read aloud by age five. That's a lot of stories, but not so many when you realize it's only one hundred per year! My grandchildren have heard thousands of stories read to them by parents and grandparents. Reading is an established routine in their home before naps and at bedtime. Each child is allowed to select one book—his or her personal favorite of the day, and then the snuggly reading begins.

But there's more to creating a learning environment in your home. The decisions begin at birth.

Will you take the time to play little rhyming games with your baby?

Will you provide board books to look at together and take the time to point out pictures while naming them?

Will you include visits to the library in your schedule? Will you attend their story hours?

Will you purchase books as birthday and Christmas gifts along with the dolls and trucks?

And here's an important one; will you read yourself, modeling the fact that reading is a wonderful part of adult life?

There are so many ways you can encourage your children to be ready for formal reading instruction. But what do they really need to know by age four or five?

Pre-reading Skills

Young children learn most of their language skills simply by exposure to language. They hear sounds and imitate them. They begin to match meaning to sounds and over time they create their own simple words and sentences. That's how they learn to speak. Learning to read is based on the same kind of exposure to the language and format of books. Learning the necessary pre-reading skills is, in great measure, "caught" rather than taught.

In the process of enjoying books at reading times, children will naturally absorb information such as left to right and top to bottom. They'll begin to notice books have titles and that illustrations are clues to the meaning of the story. They'll recognize the fact that there are lines of symbols called letters on each page and that the reader is following them, saying those words. They'll understand the words have meaning. They'll also recognize that stories have characters and action and there's a beginning, middle and end to each story. Yes, they'll learn all those things without you intentionally teaching them.

Of course you can take the opportunity to teach as you read. You can ask questions about the characters and what they may say or do. You can look for letters or words your child already knows. You can ask for predictions of endings…and so much more. There are benefits to interacting with the stories you read at more than just the surface level, but there are cautions too. You don't want daily read-alouds to become "boot camp" for learning to read later on. Don't worry; there's plenty of time for formal instruction later. You want to keep these special reading times pleasurable for everyone.

Never Too Late

I once had a friend who confided to me, *"I know I should be reading with my children, but I just don't enjoy it."* Maybe you can relate. If so, take heart because it's never too late to begin enjoying books together. I'm adding a list of pre-reading activities to enjoy with your children. Get started today because if you think of reading as hard work, your children are apt to feel that way too. Try selecting books about topics of interest. Boys often like adventure books with lots of action or non-fiction books about real things—tigers, sharks with sharp teeth or snakes. After reading about a topic your child loves, follow up with an activity which extends the fun of reading. Take a look at the list of reading-related activities in *Appendix 4* to get some ideas.

Another suggestion is to choose quality books. There are lots of "grocery store" children's books that find their way into shopping carts or are ordered through online or catalog offerings. Beware of books that are about the latest television show or cartoon character, as they tend to be written poorly and in haste for the purpose of making a lot of money. Instead look for well-known children's authors and quality writing. I've also included a list of excellent children's authors and titles to help you make your choices. (*Appendix 2 & 6*)

Reading: A Ticket to Lifelong Learning

Some children will learn to read more easily than others, but all can learn. And since reading is a skill that opens doors to learning absolutely anything in the whole wide world, it's well-worth the effort it takes to learn. Just think, you can pave the way to reading success for your children by merely spending time each day reading to them.

It isn't difficult and it doesn't cost much if you use your local library. The time spent will be rewarded richly by skills your children gain while you read a favorite story.

Books for Babies

Board books are best for babies. They can learn to hold them, turn pages, and look at the pictures and hear the words as you read them. Just like many older children, they love to hear and see the same books over and over again.

Here are some great titles:

Goodnight Moon by Margaret Wise Brown

Go, Dog, Go by P.D. Eastman

Brown Bear, Brown Bear by Bill Martin, Jr.

Runaway Bunny by Margaret Wise Brown

Dr. Seuss's ABC by Theodor Seuss Geisel

The Very Hungry Caterpillar by Eric Carle

Where's Spot by Eric Hill

Pat the Bunny by Dorothy Kunhardt

Books for Toddlers

Toddlers enjoy repeating rhymes and rhythms such as those found in nursery rhymes. They like short books with just a few words on each page. Here are some favorites:

The Poky Little Puppy by Janette Lowrey

Over in the Meadow by Ezra Jack Keats

The Snowy Day by Ezra Jack Keats

Curious George by H.A. Rey

Corduroy by Don Freeman

Red Leaf, Yellow Leaf by Lois Ehlert

The Cat in the Hat by Dr. Seuss

Books for Three and Four-year-olds

Three and four year olds can handle stories with a beginning, middle and ending. They enjoy getting to know characters and can predict what may happen.

Here are some great titles for them:

Inch by Inch by Leo Lionni

The Mitten by Jan Brett

Gingerbread Baby by Jan Brett

Winnie the Pooh by A.A. Milne

Where the Wild Things Are by Maurice Sendak

If You Give a Mouse a Cookie by Laura Numeroff

Leo the Late Bloomer by Robert Kraus

A Kiss for Little Bear by Else Minarik

Since there are literally hundreds of wonderful stories for young children, it's also good to recognize the names of great children's authors. Here are some of them:

Arnold Lobel   Mo Willems
Jan Brett   Karen Katz
Jane Yolen   Byron Barton
Kevin Henkes
Tana Hoban
Cynthia Rylant
Leo Lionni
Eric Carle
Richard Scarry
Sandra Boynton
Robert McCloskey
Ruth Krauss
Russell Hoban
Steven Kellogg

Look in *Appendix 2* to find wonderful websites that promote reading skills for young children and in *Appendix 4* for extension activities to do after reading books together.

Cracking the Code: Why Learning to Read is a Complex Process

Chapter Two

Cracking the Code: Why Learning to Read is a Complex Process

Imagine this is your big day. You've been eagerly awaiting your first lessons in a subject everyone important to you thinks is the The. Best. Ever. You walk into a room and sit down in your own special place. The teacher is friendly and encouraging and you know this will be wonderful—you're going to learn to read.

But wait, what's this? No one told you that the language you're learning is called English. The instructor proceeds to introduce you to a long line of squiggles she calls letters. Each one of these letters has two forms. These letters have sounds associated with them but in addition there are exceptions—lots of them, and you're supposed to learn them all. Your palms are beginning to sweat and even singing the song about the letters doesn't calm your fears. This reading thing is way more than you bargained for—it's scary-hard. Maybe you'll just drop the class and enroll in something easier—like rocket science.

Yes, learning to read is a complex process and if we expected our children to learn all about it in just a few lessons, we'd be failing to recognize they are entering a process that takes even the quickest of learners years to master. Luckily, most children love the process and a wise teacher will keep it that way. **Here are some of the reasons learning to read in English is so challenging:**

Twenty-Six Symbols Times Two

The English language has twenty-six letters, but most children have learned only capitals in their pre-school years. They have proudly and painstakingly written their names in all capitals only to be told as they enter school that they've been doing it wrong. Now, in their beginning reading instruction, they must master both the capitals and the lower case symbols, and match the appropriate sound with each. Throw in the alternate formations of the letters 'a' and 'g' in some texts and we have an additional opportunity to become confused.

Sound-symbol Relationships with lots of exceptions

Each letter in the English language has a sound. Some of them have several possible sounds. The vowels, for example, have two main sounds, but also have sounds based on position in a word. So, an e may say "e" as in men, or it may say "e" as in we, but it can also be silent when it comes at the end of a word. Then the letter c can either say a "k" sound or an "s" sound. And g can say a "guh" or a "juh." What's up with that? All of these exceptions are a lot to remember when those squiggles are still relatively new to the eye. But there's more.

Tricky Issues

There are letter groupings in English which entirely change the sound an individual letter or group of letters makes. For example when s and h are put together they make a digraph, creating a totally new sound. Likewise, ph, wh, ch and th. Then there are blends such as br, dr, sl, bl, etc. Though each sound is heard in a blend, the reader must recognize the pairing and read it as a unit to pronounce the word correctly. Just for fun, there are also three letter blends such as str and spl. Are your palms sweating yet?

There are a few surprises in English that probably go back to early English and all the transitions it's made from the Old English of the mother country. Name the letters w and y out loud to yourself. I think you'll agree that the letter w should, by all rules of logic say "d". But of course it doesn't. And, by the same logic, the letter y should say "w". As adults we have become so used to the standard sounds, we tend to forget these are definitely surprises to children struggling to make sense of shapes and sounds.

Word chunks are another way that sounding encounters a roadblock. While most chunks can be sounded such as ake or ack, there are chunks of letters such as ight or suffixes such as tion that must be recognized and memorized. A little reader might be half way through the i-g-h-t before recognizing that it goes together into one phoneme (sound chunk). And let's not even begin with all the sounds of ough. (Cough, rough, though, through, etc.) Homophones are another tricky challenge to reading. We have see and sea, hear and here. We have to, too and two and for, fore and four. There are many adults who have not mastered these tricky English words and their proper usage.

English has quite a few words embedded in our everyday usage that are borrowed from other languages. The Italian word confetti originally meant candy-covered nuts, but came to mean a shower of paper. The Greek word kudos meant glory and now means honor or recognition. And from Old English through the occupation of India, comes the word khaki, meaning dusty in Hindi. The addition of these words in our everyday language adds a tricky component to saying correct sounds as we read.

English is a language with many rules. Unfortunately a very large percentage of English words break these rules. The exceptions must be learned through trial and error and exposure to oral language before they become automatic. The high frequency word *come* is a classic example of a rule-breaker. By the existing rules in English it should say "comb". But then comb should say "cuh aw m b." It doesn't. Do you begin to appreciate the complexity of the task of learning to read English?

But take heart. All of us have learned to read at one level or another. It's not an impossible task. All these examples of the difficulty level and exceptions are given for just one reason—to encourage us to appreciate the enormity of the task of learning to read. It's a skill of phenomenal importance in that it opens the entire world of learning to those who master it. Of course some children seem to have an extra chip in their computer and learn with such ease that one wonders how it was done. Others have to work harder to memorize the long lists of letters, sounds, words and meanings or absorb them through speech and context (what makes sense). They have to spend more time in order to succeed. But, here's the good news. Everyone can do it.

In my thirty-five years of teaching experience there is one character trait that makes reading success most likely and that's a positive attitude. The positive attitude has to come from both the learner and the teacher. First, the child has to want to learn to read and that can be achieved by making books and reading a family constant. It's said that a child should have heard 500 books read aloud before beginning to tackle reading on his or her own. Just listening to others read plants a whole host of reading readiness skills in the child's brain. And then there's the need for guided practice, allowing room for errors and the celebration of small successes. Have you heard of the Dick and Jane readers? It's a happy day when your little reader can remember that the one starting with the capital D is Dick and the one with a J is Jane. The actual reading and sounding skills along with using other cues such as the picture will confirm that, yes, that says Dick and the other one says Jane. Time for a celebration!

While we're talking about patience and small steps in learning to read, let me put in a plug for stopping to make sense of the story. Because sounding out words is labor-intensive (it requires making lots of sound/symbol connections while also trying to get some rhythm into the process,) the serious little reader tends to focus on saying the right thing without doing a lot of thinking about the meaning. That's natural, and if you'll go back to your first day trying to remember all the squiggles in English you'll be reminded of the difficulty level of learning to read even the most basic of English texts. So let your little reader spend time sounding carefully and putting together three to five word sentences with a picture. Then take a break and talk about the story. Just who is Dick and what does Spot want? Is their home like yours? What sort of child is Jane? Begin the process of reading for meaning, because the hard work of sounding will get in the way of true understanding. Sounding has to be done, but reading is so much more than that.

If you're embarking on the teaching of reading adventure right now, I envy you. It's a wonderful experience when done with a positive attitude, love of learning and with a whole pile of patience. Celebrate the little victories for those who learn quickly and also for those who take a little more time. Remember, while learning to read may be a complex and challenging task, the rewards are amazing. A reader can take great pride in a task accomplished and can also choose to learn about anything at all in our big wide world!

Activities to Support beginning Readers:

Make those letters: Use all sorts of household supplies to "build" the letters, both capitals and lower case. You might glue macaroni noodles or buttons on cardboard, bend pipecleaners, write the letters in a shallow pan of cornmeal, rice or sand. Use playdough to shape them. Cut letters out of sandpaper and have children trace them with their fingers. All of these tactile activities build visual and spatial memory.

Cruise the News: The daily newspaper can become a treasure trove of reading fun. Hunt first for upper and lower case letters. Next hunt for high frequency words such as *the* and highlight them. Finally look for punctuation marks, vocabulary words, nouns and verbs – virtually any word or word skill you are currently teaching in your reading times.

Play Some Games: Use your stash of board games to reinforce reading skills. Play memory games using lower case and capital letters, play junior Boggle for simple spelling skills, build word family charts with all the words in the ink family, play letter or sound bingo. Set up a Post office for creating and "mailing" letters, notes, cards, etc. Many of these game materials are available in stores such as *Learning Palace* or *Learning World*.

See *Appendix 7* for a list of easy-to-gather materials for your home reading and writing center.

Bedtime Stories and More: Why It's So Important to Read Aloud to Children

Chapter Three

Bedtime Stories and More:
Why It's So Important to
Read Aloud to Children

Remember the woman who confided, *"I know I should read to my children, but I just don't enjoy it.?"* Sadly, she didn't enjoy reading herself, and she passed that feeling on to her children who missed out on one of life's greatest pleasures—the joy of reading. Research on children and reading concludes over and over again that the very best way to give children a head start in learning is to read aloud to them from the time they're born.

Here are some of the major reasons reading aloud prepares children to read and learn on their own:

1) Reading aloud with your children shows them you find books pleasurable.

You spend special time with them at naptime or bedtime and together you share fun or exciting or informative book experiences. It's a shared experience and one children enjoy immensely.

2) Reading aloud as children look on gives them important "background knowledge."

They listen while you read stories, or information about

snakes, or poems with rhythms and rhymes that make them giggle. They hear new words, and make new connections. They learn that a wealth of fun and information lies in thousands of books and someday they'll read all by themselves.

3) Reading aloud makes you a role model for literacy.

Children will naturally catch your enthusiasm as you change your voice for each character or marvel at the intricacies of butterflies or birds. If it's important and fun for you, they want to he part of it.

4) Reading aloud introduces a variety of reading experiences.

Children will begin to know the kind of books they like best. My oldest grandson prefers chapter books such as the Narnia books, while my middle grandson loves books on nature. My youngest is partial to books about dinosaurs and trucks.

5) Read alouds introduce children to "book language" which is quite different from everyday speech.

They will learn about dialogue and rhyming. They'll hear descriptive language that is beautiful to the ear and words with sounds like "Bang" and "Pop." They will anticipate what happens next in a story and get the rudiments of language which will later help them to write their ideas on paper.

6) Reading aloud fuels the creativity that resides inside each child.

> They begin to explore ideas of various people, places, times and events beyond their own little world.

7) Reading aloud opens the door to conversation about the ideas and facts encountered along the way.

> Children learn to think and respond to stories by asking questions or making comments. There is opportunity to share ideas about characters and plot which will support reading and writing skills in the future.

8) The biggest reason to read books aloud is——fun!

> Read aloud times need to be special and snuggly and enjoyable. Choose books from a variety of genres, and allow the children to make selections part of the time.

When I was a child my family enjoyed fishing on Puget Sound. The night before a fishing trip, my father brought in his tackle box from the garage and opened it as if it contained treasure. He unpacked hooks and sinkers, line and lures. He painstakingly tied leaders to lures, and rolled them up into little bundles. Then he placed them into a compartment just the right size and went on to the next. My brother and I sat at his feet, watching this magical display. We knew the next day all of these items would be used as Dad baited hooks for us and we went after the elusive salmon. It was a red letter day if we caught one. And if we didn't, we still enjoyed the time on the water and all the food we ate while sitting and holding our poles.

I tell you all of this because in my family fishing was a big deal. My parents knew it, and my brother and I did too. Lots of time went into preparation for our day trips on the bay and it was a major source of family recreation. Fish stories to tell friends and family were the norm. What my family did with fishing, you can do with reading. Moms and Dads alike can show children that reading is fun and exciting and just the best thing since sliced bread.

When to begin?

Some moms begin reading aloud even when baby is yet to be born. Studies have shown that babies respond in the womb to music, so why not to poetry or rhymes? Tiny babies respond to the sound of their mother or father's voice at an early age.

Here are some great choices for read alouds:

For Babies

- Choose sturdy board books or washable cloth or vinyl books.

- Babies love bright colors and simple pictures on solid backgrounds.

- Babies respond to rhythm in language so they love simple rhymes.

- As they get a little older, babies enjoy seeing pictures of familiar objects such as animals, food or clothing items.

- They love stories about things they do such as eating, taking a bath or going to sleep.

- When babies begin to talk they love to repeat rhymes, phrases and known words.

- Babies love to touch a variety of textures in books and help to turn pages.

- They love to read homemade books with pictures of their family members or other familiar objects.

For Toddlers

Read alouds for Toddlers will help to expand their listening skills. They'll learn new words to increase their vocabularies. They'll learn to link pictures and stories with their own life. They'll begin to create pictures in their minds while listening and they'll begin to understand print concepts such as letters, words, and illustrations.

Here are some ideas for choosing books for toddlers:

- Toddlers enjoy books that talk about their feelings.

- They love predictable patterns and repeated words or phrases.

- They like to participate when possible, touching, lifting flaps, moving and pointing.

- They need stories that are short with just a few words per page.

- They love books about size, shape, color and time.

- They enjoy books about skills they are learning such as taking a bath or brushing their own teeth.

- Toddlers love to read the same books over and over again.

- It is helpful to stop and ask questions about the pages. Where is the train? Can you find the red truck?

- Ask questions. What will the boy do? Will the baby duck find its Mama?

For Pre-Schoolers

If you've read aloud from the time a baby is born, children are old pros by the time they're pre-schoolers. They'll be able to sit and listen for a longer period of time. They'll understand that pictures support the words. They'll know when to turn a page and anticipate what comes next. They'll know there are characters in stories and stories have a beginning, middle and ending. They'll be learning their alphabet and point out some letters accurately. They'll have favorite books and topics and be invested in choosing the books for family read aloud times.

When reading aloud to pre-schoolers:

- Choose stories with characters your children relate to.

- Allow children to retell favorite stories in their own words.

- Allow them to act out stories with their stuffed animals or puppets.

- Enlarge their knowledge bases with non-fiction books on a variety of topics.

- Grow their imaginations with exposure to fables, folk tales, plays, and a variety of stories.

- Read poems with rhymes and repeated beginning sounds. (alliteration)

- Mention the book's author, illustrator, and the parts of the book such as a table of contents or a glossary.

- Find books that answer your child's questions about a topic.

- Stop and ask questions as you read, such as "What might happen next?" or "Why did she do that?"

- Allow children to do art extensions after reading, such as drawing, painting, or otherwise re-creating the story.

For Kindergarteners & Elementary School Students

Kindergarteners and primary school children will continue to enjoy read aloud times. They can absorb the information in each story, make sense of plots and understand characters. They'll become aware of writing styles and how different they can be. They'll grow their vocabularies and become good thinkers as they listen. They're anticipating the time they can read on their own and can try their hand at recognizing letters and words.

When you read with kindergarteners and primary learners:

- Choose some books they can read themselves and others they cannot.

- Introduce chapter books with clear characters and plots.

- Read longer stories with messages and morals.

- Select books related to their specific interests.

- Help them to learn about authors and begin to have favorites.

- Talk about books before reading them to help children listen for certain story lines, problems, and ways characters resolve their problems.

- Summarize a story together to get the main ideas.

- Help listeners relate to stories by asking questions such as "What would you have done?" or "Can you think of another way?"

- Compare books you've read. How are they alike and different?

I can't emphasize enough the importance of keeping read alouds enjoyable. When reading together becomes a chore, it's time to stop. Visits to a local library or book store may encourage enjoyment and participation in the listening process. Allowing children to choose books they enjoy helps build "buy in." And trust me, those children who have had hours of read-aloud enjoyment will be ready for formal reading instruction when the time comes.

By the way, don't stop reading aloud to your children as they get older. In fact families can take turns being the designated reader while everyone listens. Good books offer a lifetime of pleasure. Reading is great family fun.

Building Reading Skills:
Why it's Okay to
"Just Memorize."

Chapter Four

Building Reading Skills:
Why it's Okay to
"Just Memorize"

You and your pre-readers have doubtlessly spent countless hours poring over books. You've read nursery rhymes, fairy tales, fables, animal stories, mini-mysteries and so much more. You love reading about real-life things. You read about snakes and birds and whales. You love books.

There will come a time in your child's reading journey when he or she will begin to "tell" the stories that are favorites. Your pre-reader doesn't really know how to read the print yet, but certainly knows the story word for word. And, will tell you if you happen to miss a word or a page.

Parents often become uncomfortable during this stage of building reading skills. It seems the child is taking a shortcut to reading and maybe even cheating just a bit. No worries. This is a normal and essential part of learning all about the complicated skill we call reading.

Reading is developmental.

At an early age, as language develops, children learn sounds are part of words and that words convey meaning. As you read to your babies and later your toddlers, they begin to understand print concepts such as top and bottom of pages, left and right orientation to flow of words. They learn that clumps of letters make up words and that the words create an unlimited number of poems and stories. They relish the rhythm and rhymes so prevalent in pre-school picture books. They begin to expect a story to have characters who act in various ways. They learn that stories have problems to solve, emotions to share and that when the last page is read, there is an end to the story. All of these bits of information are essential to understanding the process of reading.

So, when your child begins to recite the book you're reading aloud, you've reached a milestone. Not only does your little pre-reader understand all of the above concepts, he or she can learn the storyline independently. Rather than think of memorization as a shortcut to "real reading," think of it as a major step toward becoming an independent, fluent reader.

Memorization of an entire story is quite a feat. Later on, when comprehension of stories will be so important to successful reading tasks, this ability to make sense of a story and relate it back to another person will serve as a feather in the reader's cap. He'll be able to do an accurate retell of a story just read. She'll be able to answer comprehension questions pulled from the text.

At the same time as children tell a story through memorization, they're beginning to understand there is one to one matching of written and oral words. When you read the word "cat," be sure to put your finger under that word. Soon children will point and touch one word at a time as you read aloud. Take the time to point out key words after reading each page. And, after finishing the book, go back and find key words again. All of these experiences with text help unlock the necessary elements to becoming a good reader.

Of course there's a time to begin learning letter names and their corresponding sounds. In fact you can work on these skills at a very early age as long as you allow the child's developmental clock to dictate when it's time to really know them. Generally a child will recognize all 26 letters sometime around age five, but I know some children who knew their letters even before they could speak full sentences, and others who needed a little more time before mastering the whole alphabet. Many opportunities to interact with words in stories give your child a head start in learning to read.

Once individual letters and later their sounds are mastered, it's time to work in earnest to decode words. Both phonics skills (sounding words) and memorization of sight words will be important. Once those skills are humming along, then strategies for making meaning of words will come into play. Visual memory will play a big part in learning to remember the shapes of letters. Story memory will build other understandings such as beginning, middle and end, characters who act in various ways, problems to be solved and maybe a lesson to be learned.

Remember that learning to read is developmental. It happens step by step. Small successes build confidence, and confidence gives children the courage to try something new, make a few mistakes and then self-correct. This is something all good readers must do. Later there will be plenty of time to build accuracy and fluency. For now the "just telling" from memory is a sign that all is well. Your child is happily traveling the road to reading.

Tips for Reading to Pre-schoolers

Before a story:

- Read the title and talk about it. What will this story be about?

- Take a picture walk. Who and what do you see?

- Preview the vocabulary. *"I see the word puppy. Do you think this story is about a dog?"*

During the story:

- Talk about the storyline. Make predictions. *"What do you think will happen next?"*

- Make note of rhymes, rhythms, special words, new words, repeated words.

- Note characters and their actions. Are they happy, sad, troubled, joyful? Why?

After the story:

- *"What did you like about this story?"*

- *"Can you find the word ___?"*

- *"What would you do if you were part of this story? Would you change anything?"*

Story times are meant to be times of enjoyment. If they "just say it from memory," they're on the road to reading "for real."

Strategies Good Readers Use

Chapter Five

Strategies Good Readers Use

As adults, most of us have reached the wonderful level of reading achievement known as automaticity. That means we seldom have to stop and "figure out" a word unless we're reading tax forms or technical writing. We just read and focus on the meaning. Some of us read quickly and some more slowly, but in general we're not even thinking about the strategies we're using—they've become automatic.

Children learning to read do need to learn strategies to use when they come to a word they don't know. It's tempting to rely only on phonics—that is sounding the letters, but unfortunately that only works about half the time in English. Italian children live in a beautiful world where every letter always makes the same sound. English speakers have a maze of exceptions to wade through. So, it makes good sense to arm our little readers with multiple ways to unlock new words.

The following are strategies readers can try when they get stuck. Each of these strategies should be modeled by adults as they read to children to reinforce their use. *('Hmm, I'll go back and reread that, or, Let's see, I know dog, could the word be doghouse?')*

They can also be taught and prompted as the child reads. This prompting usually comes in the form of a question asked when the reader has stopped to attempt a difficult word. But be careful, children need time to solve the problem on their own. Allowing "wait time" of five to seven seconds is a good way to allow children to see what they can do by themselves. After waiting, it's time to prompt the child to do some problem solving.

Eight Strategies Plus One:

1. Teach the child to read on.

Reading on means to skip the unknown word and read the rest of the sentence. The dog jumped over the table. If *jumped* is not known, the child may be able to unlock the word by reading 'over the table' and then going back to a word beginning with 'j.'

The prompt by an adult would be, *"Can you read on?"*

2. Re-reading is another skill which requires going back to the beginning of the sentence or phrase.

Children become so focused on the unknown word they often forget what has come before it. In the sentence, *The snake hissed*, it may help the reader to remind himself that this is about a snake and what a snake might do.

The prompt would be *"Go back and re-read."*

Reading professionals found that rereading is the skill most used by successful young readers.

3. Most children will automatically try the beginning sound.

This is a helpful strategy. If that doesn't give enough information, children generally look to the end of the word.

If they still don't know the word, prompt them to *"look in the middle"* and then say, *"Now let's look all the way through the word."* Using a finger to track the left to right movement is fine in early reading.

4. Try a known part.

If the reader is stuck on a long word, there is almost always a part of that word they can identify. For instance in the word *remember* the child can probably identify the beginning 're' or the final 'er.' These word chunks are very helpful in allowing the reader to do what she can for herself before getting adult help. A combination of known parts and thinking about meaning may be enough to help the reader to solve the word on her own.

The prompt: *"What parts do you know?"*

5. Teach readers to anticipate or predict.

Often this step is done before reading a story when you "take a book walk." Talk about the pictures, the characters and what might happen in this story. That sets the background of the story and helps the child anticipate the sort of words he or she might come across. It's also fine to talk about what the word might be while reading. *The chicken egg hatched on Monday.*

The prompt might be, *"What would happen to an egg?"*

6. Confirming is a strategy that helps the reader maintain confidence in his skills and learn more about phonics and spelling.

If he solved the word hatched in the previous sentence, he might look at the pictures to see if that was right. Or look back at earlier parts of the story to see if an egg hatching makes sense in the story.

A prompt for this skill might be, *"Were you right?"*

7. Use picture clues.

It seems obvious, but children do forget to look at the pictures to help them solve hard words. If the dog is jumping in the picture, then it will make sense to find the word jumping in the text. This is not cheating, it's using common sense.

The prompt: *"What do you see in the picture?"*

8. The reader needs to ask herself, "What makes sense?"

Reading is all about meaning.

When a hard word stops the flow of reading, it's important to ask questions that lead to meaning. The reader may say, *"The cat ran up the tee."*

The prompt would be, *"Does that make sense?"*

A little thought will solve the problem and the child will self-correct, The cat ran up the *'tree.'*

9. Asking for help is okay.

We call that an appeal. It's always best if the reader tries several strategies before asking, but sometimes the word is too difficult to solve at a particular reading level. It's more advantageous to just tell it and move on. You might also model a strategy that might have worked.

Learning to read is a developmental, step by step process. It happens rapidly for some, and takes lots of practice for others. Our job as adults is to guide and direct toward independence whenever possible. Asking questions instead of 'telling the word' allows reading skills to grow over time.

Check *Appendix 1* for a list of 37 word parts known as 'rimes.' Readers can solve more than 500 words by knowing and recognizing these word chunks. I've also included below a list of additional prompts to use when working with a developing reader. These prompts give the child a bit of help without doing all the thinking for him or her.

Finally, remember for a struggling reader it's very important to find some success each day and build skills slowly. Practicing a familiar book is also wonderful for developing the fluency we hope readers will attain.

There are three kinds of reading activities:

    1) Reading **to** the child
    2) Reading **with** the child
    3) Reading **by** the child.

Reading with the child means we're alongside ready to help. Reading by the child is something he or she does alone when practicing a book already read with you. It's time to do it independently. All three kinds of reading are important in developing a confident reader.

When working with your little readers, the direct instruction, the *reading with* part, is the time to use all of the above strategies whenever they fit. And don't forget to model the same strategies when you read aloud to them—they'll begin to incorporate the skills into their reading arsenal. Be generous with praise and supportive when necessary, and before you know it, your children will be fluent readers.

More Prompts for Readers:

When they're beginners:

Use your finger.

"Did you have enough words?" (causing them to say one word for each written word, 1-1 matching)

"Try ___. Did that make sense?"

"Can you find ____?"

"Try that again."

When they're self-monitoring:

"Were you right?"

"Where is the tricky word?"

"Would ___ make sense?"

"It could be ___, but look at___.
Does that sound right to you?"

"You almost got that. See if you can find where you were wrong."

When they're using several strategies:

"Check the picture."

"Does that make sense?"

"Does that sound right?"

"What's wrong with this?" (repeat what the child said)

"Do you know a word that starts with those letters?"

"What do you know that might help?" (look for a known part)

When they're self-correcting:

"Try that again."

"I like the way you worked that out."

"Can you find your mistake?"

"You're nearly right. Try that again."

When you're encouraging fluency:

"Can you read this quickly?"

"Put the words together like you're talking."

Asking Questions to Improve Reading Comprehension

Chapter Six

Asking Questions to Improve Reading Comprehension

In 2008 I spent six weeks teaching English as a Second Language at an orphanage in India. I worked with over sixty children between the ages of three and twelve. Sometimes I had them all at once, sometimes in smaller groups of about twenty. The first week I conducted classes, I did individual reading tests with a group of second standard (about age 8) children. Four or five of them read a passage orally with virtually no mistakes. My heart soared. I could actually run a reading group with these children! Alas, my soaring heart did a complete nosedive minutes later when I asked a few comprehension questions about the passage. Not one of them knew the first thing about who or what or where. They had merely learned to "say" English from the printed page.

Why Questioning Helps

Likewise, here in the states, many children learn to read aloud and sound very confident. They can see the words on the page and are able to translate the written word into the oral version. They, too, sound as if they understand what they're reading. The startling news is that for many readers, they're so busy with the decoding part of reading, learning to say it right, they aren't even able to entertain the idea of the meaning of the words. Let's say you were reading a medical journal and you came to the word "dysrhythmia". Unless you're trained in the medical field, you would first need to figure out how to say the word and then you might begin to ask yourself what it meant. You'd see rhythm and know it's something to do with regular beats. You'll know that dys probably means something is wrong and soon you'll have a good idea that this is a word about the heart beating inappropriately. You would have arrived at that understanding by asking yourself questions. Unconsciously you asked yourself questions such as, *"What do I see in this word that I already know? What could that mean? I wonder if it means...."* It's true. Good readers have learned to ask questions along the way to gain deeper and fuller understanding of the text. Most often this is an unconscious process, but children need guidance to master the skill.

Before They Read

When young children begin to learn their alphabet and recognize simple words the focus is all on visual memory. There may be clues such as recognizing the shape and color of a stop sign. It's an octagon, it's red...it says STOP. They'll learn to recognize and write their name. Then as they become curious about other words, their known vocabulary expands. When they begin reading simple sentences such as 'The cat ran fast.', they will most likely read 'the' as a sight word. They memorize the shape and the pattern of the word. When they begin to read cat, c-a-t they are looking at each letter and interpreting both the letter and its sound until the word becomes automatic for them. We introduce short vowel words or "magic e" words to open up hundreds of possibilities for the new reader. All is well as long as we don't throw in too many words with exceptions to the rules too quickly. This, we say, is reading. Now you can read a sentence.

And, for the beginner, this is reading. It's a wonderful start. But it's really only a scratching the surface kind of beginning, because true reading is making meaning. Just saying the words with little or no understanding is known as "barking at the moon." It's not really reading. When words are said and understood, then we have true reading.

Once the reading process is well on its way, and children are able to say each word correctly, we need to begin asking questions leading to meaning. We'll ask, *"What did the cat do?"* or *"How did the cat run?"* At first this will surprise the reader who is just glad to be able to say the words correctly. Must they also think about what the words are telling them? Well, yes they must. By the time a child is eight or nine years of age, he or she will read science textbooks, fairy tales about knights and dragons, mathematical story problems and so much more. It's essential that a reader think beyond saying words correctly. The strong reader asks questions to make sure meaning is in place.

Jacob loves airplanes so he selects a book off the shelf. He begins to look through the book for pictures and yes, he sees several nice pictures of airplanes, both on the ground and in the sky. Under the pictures are some words. Hmmm, the man beside the plane might be a pilot. That word, pilot, will probably be in the story. And how about other words to expect such as fly, take-off, landing and wing? And this sort of wing won't be on a bird, because this book is all about airplanes. We see that "taking a walk through the book" before actually trying to read it is a wise and worthwhile thing to do. Jacob will ask himself questions such as, *"I wonder how a pilot learns to fly?" "How fast will these airplanes go?" "Is it safe to fly an airplane?"* His questions will be about general meaning and what he can expect to find in this particular book. The questions will help Jacob get ready for the actual reading experience. Asking him to predict what will happen in this book is a good strategy for increasing his understanding as he reads.

During Reading

Today Miriam is reading a book about a princess. She has looked through the book and knows there will be a castle and a king and queen and that the princess looks sad part of the time. She has asked herself questions such as, *"Why is the princess crying?"* and *"What are the King and Queen saying to the princess?"* Now it's time to begin at the first page and read through the story.

Sometimes we become so focused on reading fluently that we hinder the reader from stopping to make sense of the meaning. There are times when it makes perfect sense to stop reading, do some questioning and thinking and be sure the meaning is coming through. Then it's good to go back and begin again for a smooth read.

On the very first page of this princess book Miriam comes to the word castle. That's a hard word because there is a silent 't' in the middle. But if Miriam has thought about her princess and seen the picture of a castle, she will probably solve the puzzle quickly. She may be in more trouble when she comes to the word moat. That is not a word commonly read by young children, but she may have the background knowledge to figure it out. If not, she'll sound it and get close. Now, she must ask herself *"What is a moat?"* Picture clues will help and then she'll need to think logically about the words nearby. If the text says, *"Don't fall into the moat."* she'll need to analyze that clue and she'll know a moat is something you could possibly fall into. If there is talk of water or fish or a bridge, she may also get a visual picture of a ditch sort of thing that goes around the castle for protection. An older child might make use of a dictionary, but sometimes the context of the story plus pictures offer the only clues to meaning for young readers.

When reading one on one with a child, it's beneficial to ask questions along the way. The questions don't always need an answer, but rather serve to direct thinking. For example in the airplane book, you might ask Jacob, *"Wow, I wonder what it feels like to be up in an airplane like that? Do you think the pilots ever feel scared?"* Or, *"What do you think all those buttons and levers and screens mean? Let's see if we can find out."* The questions direct the reader's attention to the details of the story and focus on understanding.

When the story is fiction, it's important the reader understand the action of the story. Some characters are involved. *Who are they? What do they want? Are they happy or sad? And what will they do?* Guiding questions during reading will help your child learn to ask those same sorts of questions when he or she reads independently.

After Reading

There are a number of kinds of questions to ask after reading a book. There are evaluations such as, *"Did you like this story?" "Why or Why not?" "What did you like about the main character?"* There are literal questions such as remembering the color of the girl's dress or the number of buttons on the boy's shirt. These tend to be less important questions to ask and are sometimes overused, especially for early readers when stories are quite simple. Better to ask questions that require inferences such as *"Why do you think the boy ran away? Was he scared? Was he angry?"* Such a question requires the reader to make connections from his or her own background knowledge to the character in the book. Making inferences requires higher level reflective thinking and is a better measure of true understanding.

A fun way to work on comprehension skills after reading is to "retell" the story. With practice the reader will be able to include all the important characters and the story line with a beginning, middle and an ending.

Asking Questions when Reading Independently

The goal in reading comprehension is for the reader to recognize when to ask questions for optimal understanding. As skilled readers we notice when something isn't making sense and either decide it's not important to our understanding or make an effort to solve the problem. If it's a word we don't know, we may use a dictionary. If we don't know who is speaking, we'll look back at text already read. Our questions are automatic and even subliminal at times. We want our children to practice asking themselves questions whenever meaning is lost. We also want the kind of evaluative questions that come when we've learned something new or have interacted with the story in a way that makes us think about life. *"Would I have done what Jack did when he met the giant?" "Why weren't Hansel and Gretel more afraid of that witch?"*

Remember that the reading atmosphere in your home is created by each member of the family. If you're in the habit of discussing books around the dinner table, your children will learn to think about the things they read. If your children see you reading for pleasure and information, they'll want to do that too. Interacting with the ideas in books will be the norm.

Teach your little readers to ask questions before, during and after reading. It will improve their understanding and enjoyment of every book they read.

Helping Children
Choose a
'Just Right' Book

Chapter Seven

Helping Children Choose
a 'Just Right' Book

My six-year-old grandson was spending a week with me this summer and we decided to take advantage of a read-aloud time at our local library. It's a beautiful new building with spacious aisles and thousands of books in the children's section. After listening to a great story I looked forward to a pleasant book-selecting experience.

I told my grandson he could check out some books on my card after story time. All went well as we heard several stories and participated in energetic hand motion games. But then, as we left the story room and entered the beautiful children's section of the library, I noticed some strange behaviors from my grandson. First he decided to play a little hide and seek game from one aisle to another. Then he focused on the computers and the games they offered. After we played a computer reading game we went back to the task of selecting books. A bit more foot-dragging and he finally walked over to a shelf, picked up two books, and handed them to me without even looking at their covers.

It finally dawned on me. The child had absolutely no idea how to begin choosing a good book at his own reading level. Now, he'd just finished Kindergarten in an excellent school, but when it was library time there he had a librarian to direct him to the appropriate shelves and guidance to look for his just right book.

In this new setting the sheer size of the room overwhelmed him and the rows and rows of books he can't yet read was just too much. Grandma should have taken him to one or two sections, explained his choices, and then helped him pick one or two books of interest.

It's an Art

There truly is an art to selecting appropriate books for independent reading times. You and I have skills in place that are so automatic we hardly think about them. We look at covers, open to read back cover blurbs, note the author and maybe look for a heart or a skull and crossbones to indicate a romance or a mystery. We recognize various genre through the illustrations as we look for familiar clues to the contents of our new read.

Children must learn how to choose books they will enjoy and that are appropriate for their reading level. Boys often gravitate to books on dinosaurs or baseball, girls may enjoy dress-up and fairy tales, but each child is unique, with interests that change from season to season. It's important to allow some "buy in" when children choose their reading material. In other words, we can't dictate what will be of interest to another person. We can, however, guide selections according to reading difficulty, topics, and appropriate themes.

To, With or By?

One way to think about book selections is to determine the purpose of the book. Will this book be used as a read aloud, as a teaching tool in which the child reads with an instructor, or is this an independent book to be read entirely without help? The three purposes are as different as night and day, and will determine whether or not the choice is a good one. A book read by an adult to a child can be written at a much higher level than one tackled by the child alone.

The vocabulary can be more difficult and the storyline more involved. A book to be read alone must match the child's independent reading level, and for optimal enjoyment must be a genre the child currently loves.

Young readers at a beginner level are still learning all the ins and outs of stories. They need a lot of experience just listening to adults read before tackling books on their own. They often will use the "five finger rule" of finding a just right book. If they look at a page and there are just one or two unknown words, the book is probably going to work. If there are three to five unknown words, the book is too hard to read independently.

Older readers will look for the kinds of books they most enjoy. There is a staggering selection of reading material in a public or school library. There are biographies, fantasy, folk and fairy tales, legends and myths, historical fiction and poetry. There is drama, science fiction and all manner of non-fiction material. And don't forget that newspapers, magazines, baseball cards, comics and instruction manuals are also reading material. Honor the individuality of your reader as he or she makes reading choices.

Here are some general guidelines in choosing reading material for your children, or helping them to make wise choices. It's important to remember that beginning readers feel most comfortable with books that are familiar. They love to read the same book many times and that's fine. We also want to honor the child's right to make a mistake. If a book is selected and then not read or enjoyed, this too can be a learning experience. Protecting from offensive materials and trashy quality is a different question—that's our responsibility.

Here are a few Questions to ask when Selecting Reading Materials.

1. Relevance:

Does the book relate to the child's interests, culture, language levels and, in general, their world?

2. Enjoyment:

Is the book fun, entertaining or informative?

3. Meaning:

Will the book be easily understood? Is it clear and well-written?

4. Quality:

Is the book too trivial or mundane? Is it a valuable read or a waste of time?

Will it promote satisfaction if read? Is the theme worthy and the vocabulary appropriate?

5. Variety:

Will this book broaden your child's reading horizons?

Just as adults sometimes select books for light reading, children will also choose books for sheer entertainment. But it's important to challenge your readers to expand their reading experiences and try some of the Classics or do further reading in a certain genre to build skills. Reading comprehension is one of the most important skills your children will need to succeed in higher learning, so selecting books with an intricate plot, complex characters, and a story filled with rich vocabulary will help to develop deeper understanding.

A home library is a good resource for learning, but public libraries offer selection not possible within a family budget. Take advantage of your local lending libraries and teach your children how to choose good books. It's a wonderful skill to hone, and the more familiar children become with a wide variety of reading materials, the better and more accomplished learners they'll become.

Criteria for Selecting Appropriate Books

1. Subject matter:

What is the book about?

Is it appropriate for the reader's interests?

Is it understandable?

2. Storyline:

Is the story engaging and does it teach a lesson or carry an appropriate theme?

Does the story entertain, teach, inform?

Is it a worthwhile story?

3. Word Patterns and Vocabulary:

Is the level of reading appropriate for your reader?

Is it too hard, too easy?

Are there an appropriate number of words on each page?

Do the pictures add information and support the storyline?

4. Density of Information/Text Organization:

Especially for non-fiction books, is there an appropriate amount or combination of words, pictures, labels, etc. on each page?

If there is too much information, or if it is poorly organized on the page, the reader will be overwhelmed and not able to access the information easily.

Evaluating Your Child's Reading Skills

Chapter Eight

Evaluating Your Child's Reading Skills

In the days of Dick and Jane, little readers with a lot of confidence did a good job of reading aloud for all to hear. They sat at the reading table with their group and waited for their turn to show their stuff. Those with reading issues often hated this public display of their inability to perform. In independent work times children were given workbooks with questions related to the day's story. If they could read the questions and correctly select one of three answers they were good readers. If they weren't able to read the questions, they had poor comprehension scores even if they actually knew the answers.

Reading instruction has improved over time and we now know there are a variety of ways to evaluate reading ability. We have better ways of gathering reading comprehension information than blanks in workbooks. We observe readers to gather information on a variety of skills that must all be in place before reading is automatic.

How can you tell if your child is making satisfactory progress in reading skills? There are literally hundreds of ways to evaluate a child's reading, and you may be overwhelmed by all the forms and tests. Here are four components of good reading. You'll want to see how well your child is doing in each of them. This is not a scientific evaluation method, but instead common sense information from a long-time teacher of young readers.

Reading Accuracy

When children read aloud for others, there is often a bit of nervousness attached to the experience. It's a good idea to have your children read aloud for a few minutes each day to build up confidence and overcome any fears. Once that becomes routine, sit with your reader and listen. Are they reading each word accurately? Skilled teachers often do reading analyses called running records in which they take note of each error as a child reads. They also take note of the kinds of errors made. Do errors come at the beginning, middle or end of the word? Do they significantly change the meaning of the sentence or are they the "little words" such as 'the' and don't really affect understanding of the big ideas? You may find consistent errors related to a certain blend or digraph. For instance the reader may miss words beginning with sh or br because they don't know that sound yet. Early readers may mispronounce a letter such as 'w' because of sound/letter confusion. Once you identify these problems you can practice them in a separate lesson.

Reading accurately is just one of the ways we evaluate reading skill, but it's an important one. Making many accuracy errors will almost certainly reduce comprehension. It's hard to make sense of a story if dinosaur becomes dinner or if came becomes camp. Often children catch their own mistakes and go back to self-correct. This should be encouraged in the process of building reading accuracy. However it may be better to slow down and read more deliberately if too many errors are being made.

Fluency

Fluency in oral reading is all about the way the reader sounds. Does he read smoothly or are the words choppy? Does she anticipate the way words should sound when a question is asked or when the words indicate excitement? Does the reading sound natural or is the voice a monotone? Think of listening to an actor on the stage. Can you understand each word and does the meaning come across clearly? A good reader sounds as if they're speaking to a friend.

Fluency is important because it's an indicator that everything is "a go." There are no barriers in the way. The reader is picking up all the appropriate cues and is able to put correct emphasis on each word. They know when to make the tone go up as in *"Is it time?"* They know when to raise volume as in *"I'm so excited!"* Fluency also allows the reader to maximize understanding—a major goal in reading skills.

Reading Rate

Reading rate may be one of the most misunderstood and improperly taught reading skills. The tendency is to encourage children to read as fast as they can. They're even given time tests to try to increase their rate. For those children with above average reading ability, such tests may be motivating. But for average readers or those with reading challenges, trying to read fast is a disaster. First of all, rushing through reading will increase errors. Secondly and more importantly, reading quickly will almost certainly decrease comprehension because "fast" is the goal, instead of being aware of the meaning of each word. Even accomplished readers may not want to read ever faster. And what's the hurry? Aiming for smooth delivery at a reasonable rate should be the goal. Taking the occasional timed test will give some information on reading ability, but in my opinion reading rate should be de-emphasized.

Understanding

Reading comprehension is the big daddy of reading skills. If we don't understand what we read, all is lost. There is a message in the words and there are layers of meaning, some more subtle, but still important. Is the character good or bad? How can you tell? Is there a problem to be solved? Have the characters learned a lesson? The enjoyment that comes with reading is directly related to the reader's level of understanding. Strong readers begin to make inferences as they read. They figure out that the main character is selfish or foolish without being told directly. They guess that the children will fall into trouble when they disobey their parents. They are actively engaged in the ideas of the story and aren't focused on each individual word. They have become automatic in their reading skills so they're free to think about meaning. That's the goal. We want our readers to move beyond memorizing the color of the girl's dress and begin to think about her as a person. We want him to think about the story line rather than focus on isolated vocabulary words.

Reading comprehension only happens when many other skills have been mastered. All the little pieces work together into one tapestry. The reader is accurately decoding every word. The words are read smoothly, either in the reader's head or aloud, and the rate of reading matches the demands of the story. It's like a well-oiled machine. It's a beautiful thing.

Next Time you Listen to your Child Read Aloud:

● **Make a note of the errors made.**

Where do they occur in the word?

What sounds are being misread?

Are words left out or added?

Does it sound as if the reader understands what he or she is reading?

Determine the types of errors being made and then work on necessary skills in a separate lesson.

- **Have your reader do a "retell" after reading a story or a section of a story.**

Look for the big ideas of character, setting, and the sequence of action that occurs in the story. If your child can tell the story back to you with all the big ideas in place, comprehension is good.

- **Have your reader draw a picture of the story.**

What happens first, second, third?

Who are the characters and what are they doing?

How does the story end?

- **Encourage children to rewrite the story with a different ending or with different characters.**

How would the story change?

- **Get several children to act out a scene from the story or make puppets to do the job.**

Kids love to ham it up.

- **For a struggling reader, be sure to take the stress out of reading times.**

  Take turns reading or allow the reader to repeat after you.

  Practice reading smoothly and accurately or make a list of tough words or sounds to work on at a different time.

  Short but fun reading times are best.

- **Slow and steady wins the race.**

  Don't force fast reading. Instead focus on understanding and enjoying the text.

- **Work with your reader to write short stories with family members or pets as the main characters.**

  Get into the fun of creating a story. This will encourage reluctant readers to enjoy the process and they'll love reading that story over and over again.

Retelling a Story: A Great Way to Measure Comprehension

Chapter Nine

Retelling a Story: A Great Way to Measure Comprehension

Your young reader is doing great. He can read whole sentences, even paragraphs, with accuracy and confidence. You breathe a sigh of relief that this child has finally "got it." Be careful. Reading all the words correctly and with all the right ups and downs of inflection is only half the battle—or maybe even less than half. The ultimate goal in the reading quest is meaning.

Does she understand what she reads? Is he following the story line or just saying words in the correct order with no real understanding of meaning? In my thirty-plus years of teaching children to read, I regularly had children who read aloud beautifully, but had almost no comprehension of the text. How can this be?

Several Things May be Taking Place:

1. The early focus on decoding or "unlocking" words that marks early reading lessons slows the reading process down and requires focus at the word level, not at sentence or paragraph level. It's hard to think about meaning when you're just trying to figure out how to read e-n-o-u-g-h.

2. Some children have a better "ear" for the rhythms of words than others. This is a good thing but may mask a lack of comprehension. When they read, they're able to make their voice go up and down, loud and soft, at the appropriate times. This skill is sometimes called prosody and it does require a measure of understanding. You only raise your voice when reading "Stop!" if you understand the word and the exclamation mark together convey a sense of urgency. But even so, many readers who sound great when reading aloud don't know why the princess couldn't sleep on the pea or are unable to discuss the sequence of events leading Hansel and Gretel into the forest.

3. Some readers just haven't yet learned they *should* be thinking about all the elements of a story. They're merely going through the motions, getting from point A to point B and aren't particularly trying to remember facts, look for clues, make inferences based on actions and the like. Nobody told them they had to think while reading! (*Let me stop here to say there is little value in remembering facts such as the color of Cinderella's dress. It is important, however, to understand that Cinderella is a rags to riches character and that goodness overcomes evil.*) If you have a reader who sounds quite fluent but still struggles with grasping the meaning of a story, the reason may be one or all three of the above problems. No matter the reason for a lapse in comprehension, retelling a story will build comprehension skills.

Elements of a Retell

Retelling a story can be done either orally or in written form. Either way you'll look for four major elements. Each element, when woven properly into the retell, shows the degree to which the reader grasped meaning while reading.

● **Character(s)**

Does your reader know who the main characters are and what they're like?

Could she draw a picture of them or know the way they would speak?

Are supporting characters mentioned and are their roles understood? For example, what sort of person is Jack's mother in Jack and the Beanstalk? How does she affect Jack's choices and actions?

● **Setting**

Where does the story take place and how does it affect the story? Is it "one day," "one dark night" or "somewhere in outer space?"

How does the setting help set the tone of the story?

How does it influence the vocabulary used?

● **Sequential Actions**

Can your reader tell the story in the correct order of events? What happened first, next and last? Every story has a beginning, middle and end. Each part of the story has predictable action. Children learn to recognize the drama of a story from the introduction of the characters, to some problem that arises and then the choices made to reach a logical or perhaps a surprising ending.

● **Resolution**

The conclusion is not just "the end," but a place to think about the success or failure of the characters. We see ways in which they grew or changed and make judgments such as what they could have done differently, as in *"What do you think Hansel and Gretel might do next time they see a house made of candy?"*

The conclusion is a time to tie up loose ends of the story.

What was this story all about—what is the theme?

Don't Panic

Retelling stories is just one way to measure understanding. Good readers usually learn to retell major elements of a story concisely and accurately. Some children allow their imaginations to embellish the story and "make it their own." Not to worry. They don't know we're judging their comprehension; they're just taking the story in a new direction.

As your reader matures, so will his or her level of understanding. Your role is to guide, encourage and challenge him with questions that require thought, and stretch her with "I wonders," "What ifs" and other questions to gently nudge toward interaction with the text. Remember that reading is all about understanding. Retelling a story is one excellent way to gauge that understanding.

Choosing High Interest Books for Reluctant Readers

Chapter Ten

Choosing High Interest Books
for Reluctant Readers

I'll admit it, I'm afraid of math. It scares me, makes me feel inadequate, reminds me of countless past failures and tends to expose one of my most vulnerable life areas—fear of embarrassment. Luckily, reading and writing always came easily to me. Strong reading skills, a quiet disposition, and an occasional friend to supply math answers kept my report cards on the plus side.

But what if I'd been a whiz at math yet a poor reader?

What if reading aloud in front of my friends had given me the heebie-jeebies? Let me tell you—I would have learned to fear reading, I would have built walls to protect myself from embarrassing reading settings and I most certainly would not have enjoyed reading on my own.

Sadly, many children feel they've missed the reading boat and have been left behind their peers. They see reading as a threatening chore, not a joy. They'll choose any other activity before they tackle a book. And, most likely they're being asked to read "baby books" which is a further assault on their self-confidence.

Here's Some Good News.

Publishers have recognized the need for high interest books written at lower skill levels. Challenged readers no longer have to be embarrassed by books far below their age and interest levels. These high interest books tend to be non-fiction books about real topics such as space, or robots or the Knights of the Round Table. Struggling readers don't need to be subjected to tired primers that begin, "The cat sat on a mat."

Boy Stuff

Boys, even boys who are average readers, have traditionally had a difficult time finding books they love. They're looking for adventure and action. They want heroes who save the day, not fluffy kittens with bows around their necks. If you have a son who needs new reading challenges, look into high interest stories or comic books, maps, atlases or travel brochures – anything real to put a little zip into reading selections. After all, much of work-related adult reading is not stories, but instead informational reading, charts, graphs and the like.

Choice is a Great Motivator.

Once your reader has found material he or she loves, that is the time to reinforce good reading skills. Take that book about robots and practice reading it fluently. Try echo reading (you read, he reads the same sentence) to gain accuracy and take the time to talk about the terms, photos, labels, charts and graphs—whatever the text offers. You might even write your own story. Does he talk about Batman or Spiderman? Let him tell you a superhero story, jot it down and then use that as his reading text. He'll be invested in that homegrown story and will enjoy practicing it using good reading strategies and skills.

You'll be surprised at how engaged your reader becomes when the topic is perfect for his interests.

Take the time to find reading websites your child loves. They'll guide reading choices when you're at the library or bookstore. They'll help you recognize good stories for all ages and reading levels. And most of all, they'll send the message that reading is fun.

Discouraged readers may have built barriers around themselves to protect from the embarrassment and shame of reading poorly in front of others. They may be convinced they'll never get it and fear having to read "baby books." High interest, low skill books may be just the answer. Find out where you can find the perfect reading material for your reluctant reader.

You'll find listings of High Interest titles and publishers as well as websites in *Appendix 8.*

Ten Easy Ways to Make Reading More Fun

Ten Easy Ways to Make Reading More Fun

Reading is primarily a passive act physically, although our minds should be firing on all cylinders as we track a storyline. But children enjoy following up a reading session with some action.

One of the most successful series of reading lessons ever done in my first grade classroom occurred when we read The Wizard of Oz as a read aloud and the children expressed a desire to "build Oz." They used colored clay as their basic medium and even the most wiggly, reading-resistant kids in the class immersed themselves in the project. For days they planned and mapped on paper, they labeled and embellished the North, South, East and West of Oz. They created the City of Oz, all in green, smack in the middle. They acted out sections of the story and wrote dialogue for major characters. What a wonderful time they had with that story.

Whenever a good book captures your reader's imagination, don't miss the opportunity to extend the reading enjoyment in some tangible way. After all, the physical act of reading is a means of gaining information, entering a new reality, and interacting with new characters and places. All those newfound friends in their settings and situations just beg for the chance to "become real."

Allow Your Readers to Extend the Reading Experience in one of the Following Fun Ways:

1. Make a story web, graph or chart to explore the elements of the story.

Visually organizing characters, setting, and events will help to analyze the content of the story. There are literally hundreds of ways to "map" a story.

See *Appendix 5* for some ideas.

2. Create a mural.

Allow children to work independently or in small groups to depict the story. A chapter book may require focus on just one story segment or a series of pictures.

Listen to children talk about the content of the story as they plan their mural. You'll gain great insight into their understanding as you listen.

3. Ask your reader to rewrite the story for a younger child and illustrate it.

Children love to be helpers. Selecting a simpler vocabulary and writing a modified version of the text will challenge your reader to make decisions based on his or her understandings of the story.

4. Ask your child to examine the events and theme of the story.

You might provide a prompt such as, *"Tell about Dorothy's adventures on the road to Oz,"* or *"What did Dorothy learn about the great wizard?"*

"How would you have felt when...?"

5. Choose a story with lots of dialogue and act it out.

You could use traditional drama or do a reader's theater in which the child sits before the audience and reads the dialogue. Children will enter into the world of the story as they portray the characters. They'll explore the role each character plays in each event of the story. They'll be more aware of skills such as determining important details and, let's be honest, they will love hamming it up in front of an audience.

Another version of dramatic play is puppet theater. Once again, children love the process of bringing a character to life and performing. There are literally hundreds of kinds of puppets.

For ideas on puppet-making see *Appendix 4*.

6. Challenge your child's writing skills by asking her to rewrite the story with a different ending.

How would a different ending change the character's actions? The lessons learned? The events?

7. Create an artistic response to the story.

You might choose a diorama, a mobile, a 3-D scene or a collage of characters and events.

8. Make your own story-related jeopardy game.

Begin by creating categories and then write the answers to specific questions under each category. Use 3 x 5 cards taped to poster board. They can be easily turned as you play the game. Much of the learning takes place in the creation of the categories and questions, but hours of fun will take place playing the game.

9. Find another story in the same genre and do a comparison.

Fairy tales and fables work well for this exercise.

Chart the characters and their traits.

What is similar, what is different?

How do the differences affect the story line?

10. Do a word study.

This may sound dull, but some children love to hunt for specific language in a beloved story and they can learn a lot about reading and writing as they:

List all the action words (verbs).

List all the descriptive words & the nouns they describe.

Find unfamiliar words and look up their meaning.

Choose ten spelling words and quiz a friend.

Select favorite sentences and tell why you like them.

"Is it funny? Is it beautiful?"

Find similes, metaphors, compounds, synonyms, antonyms, etc.

As you can see from the list above, the choices for reading extensions are endless. You'll often get your inspiration for a project from your child's reactions to the book or the questions asked during discussions. Is there a superhero? Maybe a comic strip is a great way to summarize the story. Are the characters vastly different from one another? How about illustrating each character and list his or her role in the story?

The goal of reading extensions is always to go deeper into meaning. As children grow and mature, their understanding of the elements of the story will be reflected in the way they depict the characters, action and setting. You may be surprised to learn that readers who still struggle with the written word can blossom and shine when given alternative ways to depict their understandings.

Discouraged readers will throw themselves into an extension or project which is more than filling in a blank. Let them use their art ability to interact with the text. Let them enjoy the story through budding theater skills. Use reading extensions to both encourage your reader and accomplish valuable study of the reading material.

Keep Them Reading Over the Summer & Other School Breaks

Chapter Twelve

Keep Them Reading Over the Summer & Other School Breaks

When summer comes around with its tantalizing warm days, both parents and children breathe a sigh of relief. Everyone deserves a break from the busy schedule of school. So enjoy sleeping a little later, relaxing a little more and enjoy those beautiful summer days with plenty of outdoor fun and some good old-fashioned laziness. **But don't forget one important thing:** children, especially younger school-aged children, need to keep on reading during summer months or they'll forget many of the reading skills they learned in the last school year.

Maybe your children are the lucky ones—those who learned to read as easily as waking up each morning, but most children aren't so fortunate. They need to practice reading skills regularly because if they don't, they lose them. Can you remember how long a summer vacation used to seem? When June came along there was an impossibly long series of days and weeks before it was time for school again. Summer vacation, several months, is a very long time for a young learner. So be aware and be wise and make sure your children practice their reading skills regularly over the summer months.

Here Are Some Tips to Make Summer Reading Fun & Rewarding.

1) Plan a family reading challenge over the summer months.

When my own children were young, we brainstormed a series of rewards to be earned during the summer. We set a few guidelines such as minutes read per day or books per week and when we were successful in reaching that goal, they earned their reward.

The weekly rewards were small ones such as stickers or small toys or maybe an ice cream cone. But the big reward came at the end of the summer if we met the requirements.

That big reward might be a trip to the beach or an overnight party with friends.

Be sure to make a chart and post it where it is visible. Then block out a time each day when reading is the thing to do.

Make allowances for illness or company or other unforeseen events, but don't allow too many interruptions or your program will fly out the window like most New Year's resolutions.

2) Your local library may have a summer reading program complete with theme and lots of incentives.

If so, you're in luck. Make weekly visits to the library to enjoy their story times, check out new books and meet the requirements set by the children's librarian. You may want to add to their program so that reading daily is still the goal.

Once again, the best way to improve reading skills is by reading more often and longer. Give individual support as needed. Listening to a book read by an adult or older child also counts. Reading is reading.

3) More and more local bookstores are getting in on the summer reading program trend.

Check out your local stores to see if they have ways to encourage young readers. They may have a story hour, a theme-related program or may focus on a certain series of children's books and plan fun activities related to the selections.

4) There are a very large number of children's reading websites available online.

Many of the games and activities on these sites are as good as reading a book. They'll give practice in sounds and letters, provide listening practice, encourage reading for meaning and a whole host of other reading skills.

Choose those sites that feature quality literature and those in which the games are truly reading-related and not just chasing a character around a screen. Here are listings of excellent children's reading websites. You can preview them before allowing your children to spend time with them. Find the listings in *Appendix 3.*

5) Children's authors often have websites to promote their books.

>Some of these sites are a wealth of information, crafts, reading games and more. Take note of favorite authors as you interact with your children at reading times, and then look by name for their websites.

>**www.janbrett.com** and **www.kevinhenkes.com** are two I would recommend for younger children. You'll find more as you search for them. See *Appendix 2.*

6) Another great family reading idea is to choose a chapter book the entire family can enjoy and do a family read-aloud.

>Books such as *Where the Red Fern Grows* or C.S. Lewis's *Chronicles of Narnia* make for hours and hours of family enjoyment.

>Make some popcorn, gather in the living room or around the kitchen table and take turns reading aloud.

>Or use driving time during vacations to listen to books on tape or enjoy read-alouds. Children will remember these special family times and be exposed to great literature at the same time.

7) Parents, be readers yourself.

>There is nothing more powerful to your children than setting an example of the good reading habits you want them to develop.

When it's reading time for them, try to arrange your day so you can enjoy a book as well. Or if that isn't possible, let them see you select books from the library and enjoy them as you have time.

Talk about the books you read.

"What did you enjoy?"

"Was it the characters, or the action or the theme of the book?"

"Did the story make you think about choices people have to make or did it make you laugh?"

The world of books is filled with enjoyment and it's part of parenting to pass that knowledge on to our children.

8) Adults often take part in book clubs.

If you've been a member of a book club, you know all about selecting a book, reading a portion of it and then gathering to discuss the ideas. Sometimes readers set personal goals such as researching the author or the setting of the book. Snacks and treats go along with book club gatherings.

Why not create a family or neighborhood reading club for the kids? Make it a fun time and one that all involved look forward to each week. Give the group a name and plan an outing when the book is completed.

Sometimes art projects are a good way to extend the reading or perhaps a skit or play. The possibilities are endless and your children will see reading as an enjoyable way to spend time with friends.

Summary

So there you have it. The big truth is that reading over the summer is really important for young readers. Luckily, doing the reading can be a ton of fun. Don't allow all the hard-won reading skills earned in the past school year to become rusty or forgotten over the summer.

Find ways to make reading practice truly fun, even exciting. Your enthusiasm for summer reading will set the tone for your children.

Grab those books and enjoy!

Appendix Contents

Appendix I

Onsets, Rimes, Word Chunks and Word Families..........................113

Appendix II

Best Children's Author Websites..117

Appendix III

Best Reading Websites for Children....................................121

Appendix IV

Activities to Extend Reading Experiences...........................127

Appendix V

Sample Story Maps and Other Graphic Organizers.........................131

Appendix VI

Award Winning Books..135

Appendix VII

Materials for Your Home Reading Center.........................139

Appendix VIII

High Interest, Controlled Vocabulary Books
for Struggling Readers...143

Appendix IX

Discussion Groups...149

Notes for Group Discussions...151

Notes for Discussion Leaders..153

Homegrown Readers Discussion Questions.......................161

Feel free to contact me with your questions, problems or
reports of great reading growth.

Jan Pierce, M.Ed.
www.janpierce@comcast.net
www.janpierce.net

Onsets, Rimes, Word Chunks & Word Families

Appendix 1

Onsets, Rimes, Word Chunks & Word Families

Onsets

Onsets are word parts that come at the beginning of a word. They may be blends, in which each letter is heard, or digraphs, in which the letters make a new sound together. Children will learn to read the onset 'bl' with the rime 'ack' to make the word black.

Here is a list of English blends and digraphs.

Blends			Digraphs
br	sc	scr	ch
bl	sk	spr	ph
cr	sl	str	sh
cl	sm		th
dr	sn		wh
fl	st		
fr	sw		
gl	tr		
gr	tw		
pl	wa		
pr			

Rimes

     Words are broken into onsets and rimes. The onset comes before the first vowel, such as 'bl' in the word black. The rime is the part that comes after the onset, 'ack' in black. If a child learns the rime 'ack,' he can also read back, tack, rack and lack.

With the following thirty-seven rimes, over five hundred words can be learned. Use the rimes for "word family" practice.

Rimes					
-ack	-ink	-ate	-unk	-in	-ay
-ame	-op	-est	-ain	-ir	-ick
-at	-ump	-ill	-ank	-or	-ine
-ell	-all	-ip	-aw	-ake	-ock
-ight	-an	-ore	-ice	-ap	-uck
-ale	-ash	-eat	-ide	-ing	-oke
-ug					

Best Children's Author Websites

Appendix 2

Best Children's
Author Websites

A good author website is a valuable reading tool. It introduces you to the author on a personal and professional basis. It highlights all of their work and will draw the child in to interact with the site in some way.

The best sites have games, puzzles, videos and much more to enhance learning and enjoyment of the author's stories.

Here are some of the best author websites:

Best Author Websites

www.janbrett.com	www.mowillems.com
www.eric-carle.com	www.robertmunsch.com
www.sharoncreech.com	www.lauranumeroff.com
www.RoaldDahl.com	www.ReadKiddoRead.com
www.judyblume.com	www.pilkey.com
www.dianedegroat.com	www.timewarptrio.com
www.tomie.com	www.patmora.com
www.kevinhenkes.com	www.JackPrelutsky.com
www.willhobbsauthor.com	www.MemFox.net
www.aghines.com	www.PatriciaPolocco.com
www.jeanmarzollo.com	

When your child treasures a favorite book, take the time to find the author's website. Readers are inspired by learning more about the writing process, how the illustrations came to be and learning that real people write books. And, it's fun.

A.L.A. link to all children's authors:

The **American Library Association** is a great resource for all things related to children's literature. Find a listing of all children's authors there. *www.ala.org*

Appendix 3

Best Reading
Websites
for Children

Appendix 3

Best Reading Websites
for Children

Good reading websites bring literature to life on the screen. Many sites read the story aloud to children. They also have beginning reading games that are both educational and fun. They may offer color sheets or other printables, e-cards to make and send, have reading contests and competitions and offer recommendations on new books available. Time spent on a good reading website will help to establish the good reading skills your child is learning at home and at school.

Terrific Sites for Toddlers & Preschoolers

www.peterrabbit.com
www.pbs.kids.org/Arthur
www.speakaboos.com
www.rif.org/leadingtoreading/en/
www.janbrett.com
www.eric-carle.com
www.clickmagkids.com
www.readingbear.com
www.starfall.com
www.funbrain.com
www.teacher.scholastic.com/clifford
www.storytimeforme.com

Sites for School Kids

www.kidsreads.com
www.pbskids.org
www.smories.com
www.goodsitesforkids.org
www.storytimeforme.com
www.timeforkids.com
www.funbrain.com
www.mrsp.com
www.storylineonline.net
www.mightybook.com
www.pbskids.org/lions (Between the Lions)
www.bbc.co.uk/bitesize
www.wegivebooks.org
www.andersenfairytales.com
www.gigglepoetry.com
www.storyplace.org
www.readingrockets.org
www.readworks.org
www.abcya.com
www.bookadventure.com
www.storynory.com

Just for Boys

Boys can get left in the shuffle when it comes to reading. They want heroes and lots of action in their reading. Or they want humor. They get tired of stories about dolls and kittens.

Here are a few reading websites just for boys.

Just for Boys

www.guysread.com (find the boys' section)

www.gettingboystoread.com

www.tikatok.com (requires a subscription— a site to create books)

www.BoysLife.org

Activities to Extend Reading Activities

Appendix 4

Activities to Extend
Reading Activities

When children have enjoyed a book for its characters, exciting or funny storyline or its unique story world, they enjoy "doing something" with the pictures in their mind. Here are some examples of fun extensions you can do easily at home to make reading even more fun.

Reading Activities

- Sing nursery rhymes and other songs related to the stories.
- Act out the story with funny voices.
- Clap the rhythms of certain sentences or phrases.
- Make puppets of the main characters.* (p. 130)
- Draw a picture of the story.
- Retell the story in your own words.
- Use building blocks and stuffed animals to act out the story.
- Tell favorite stories out loud when driving in the car.
- Change the ending of a story.
- Tape record the story for listening fun.
- Create dioramas, mobiles, 3-D replicas.

Helpful Puppet Making Websites:

www.easy-child-crafts.com
www.daniellsplace.com
www.enchantedlearning.com
www.wikihow.com (click 'Make Puppets')
www.freekidscrafts.com (click 'School Days')

You Tube: 'How to Make a Sock Puppet'

Sample Story Maps & Other Graphic Organizers

Appendix 5

Sample Story Maps
& Other Graphic Organizers

Graphic organizers provide a visual structure to help remember and understand important parts of a story. They may focus on the plot, the characters, relationships between characters, important facts or concepts. They may look like a T or a circle or a web. They may have a series of boxes to chart information such as beginning, middle and end.

There are good reasons to use such graphs and charts. They provide practice in remembering. The most important reason is their proven use in developing better comprehension of stories. If a child takes the time to chart the actions of each character in a visual way, he'll understand the story better. If she compares the character traits of two main characters, she'll know more about them.

There are hundreds of ways to organize material from a story. Each is designed to pull out information from a story or book and place it in a visual representation designed to enhance meaning.

To quickly understand the use of graphic organizers, just go to one of the sites below. Teachers make great use of these handy charts and visuals. They know it works. It will work at home too and most children enjoy doing them.

You'll find free printables at the following sites. And, once you see the graphs, they're easy to make at home. Go to each site and click on graphic organizers. You'll find charts such as cause and effect, compare/contrast, timelines, sequence charts, new vocabulary organizers and much more.

Sites for Story Maps & Graphic Organizers

www.educationoasis.com

www.teach-nology.com

www.enchantedlearning.com

www.eduplace.com (also available in Spanish)

Appendix 6

Award Winning
Books

Appendix 6

Award Winning Books

The two top awards given to children's books in the U.S. are The Newbery Award for literature and the Caldecott Award for best illustrations.

The John Newbery Medal

Given by the the *Association for Library Service to Children*, an arm of the *American Library Association*, this award is given annually. It was named for John Newbery, an 18th century publisher of children's books. The first award was given in 1922. Additionally, one to five Newbery honor books are selected each year.

Books you may recognize as Newbery winners include *The Voyages of Dr. Doolittle* by Hugh Lofting, *Rabbit Hill* by Robert Lawson, *Island of the Blue Dolphins* by Scott O'Dell and *Mrs. Frisby and the Rats of NIMH* by Robert C. O'Brien.

The Randolph Caldecott Medal

Given for most distinguished American picture book for children, this award was named for Randolph Caldecott, a 19th century English artist and illustrator. The first Caldecott Award was given in 1937. You may recognize Chris Van Allsburgh's

Polar Express, William Steig's *Sylvester* and the *Magic Pebble* and Ezra Jack Keats' *A Snowy Day*, all Caldecott winners.

You can find complete lists of **Caldecott** and **Newbery Award** winning books at ***www.ala.org***.

Parents' Choice Awards

Parents' Choice Awards were begun in 1978 as a service to parents making media choices for their children. The awards cover not only books, but also toys, music, magazines, video games and websites. The awards are given by a panel of educators, scientists, artists, parents and children. The award levels are gold, silver, recommended and approved. A **Classic Award** is given to a product that has won gold approval for five years or more. See more at ***www.parents-choice.org***.

Children's Choice Awards

A relatively new program, the **Children's Choice Awards** are selected by children and teens. These awards are sponsored by the **Every Child a Reader** program, a non-profit arm of the Children's Book Publishers. Awards are voted online in K-2, 3-4 and Teen categories. There are also author and illustrator of the year awards given.

Find more information at ***www.ccbookawards.com***

For a complete listing of awards given for children's books go to ***www.readingrockets.org*** and search ***Award Winning Kids' Books***.

Materials for
Your Home
Reading Center

Appendix 7

Materials for Your Home Reading Center

Reading and writing is serious "grown up" behavior. Your children will want to do as much reading and writing as they can, as early as they can. Set up a small reading and writing center and supply it with items to encourage its use. One day it can be a post office, another an art station to draw pictures of Curious George. When you decide to extend a reading time, the center will be ready. Save boxes, plastic jars, cardboard, etc. to store the items neatly.

Resources

- *Alphabet Chart*
- *Children's Dictionary*
- *Flash Cards of all kinds*
- *Magnetic Letters and a Cookie Sheet*
- *Magazines for Pictures and finding letters and sounds*
- *Mini-chalkboards and Chalk, a Small Rag for erasing*
- *Newspapers*

Art Supplies & Creative Materials

- *Alphabet Cereal*
- *Colors, Markers, Pens, Pencils,*
- *Envelopes*
- *Lots of Paper*
- *Pipe Cleaners*
- *Play Dough*
- *Rice, Cornmeal (create letters & words with fingers)*
- *Scotch Tape, Masking Tape*
- *Paper Bags & Tubes*
- *Paper Plates & Cups*
- *Cardboard*
- *Straws*
- *Fabric Scraps & Ribbon*
- *Yarn & String*
- *Rubber Stamps & Pads*
- *Stickers*
- *Sticky Notes*

Child-Safe Necessary Tools

- *Child-safe Scissors*
- *Glue and Gluesticks*
- *Rulers*
- *Staplers and Staples*
- *Brads Paper Clips*
- *Paper Clips*

High Interest, Controlled Vocabulary Books for Struggling Reader

Appendix 8

High Interest, Controlled Vocabulary Books for Struggling Reader

If learning to read has been difficult, children may have built barriers to the entire process. To make matters worse, they may be ten years old, but reading at a level that is still stuck on short vowel sentences: The cat sat on the mat. Not very much fun.

Luckily there are lots of books written with high interest and a controlled vocabulary. They tend to be non-fiction books with lots of information, pictures, labels and charts and graphs or fiction stories with a high degree of action and age-appropriate themes.

Your local librarian will be able to help you find high interest books, sometimes called "hi-lo" books. They come with a reading level plus an interest level. For example an Orca book called *Beyond Repair,* by Lois Peterson about a teen-aged boy who has lost his father is rated 2.5-4.5 reading level, but has an interest level for readers aged ten through fourteen.

Here is a listing of publishers who have hi-lo books available on their websites:

Publishers of 'Hi-Lo' Books

Bearport Publishers: www.bearportpublishing.com

Orca Publishers: www.orcabook.com

High Interest Publishing: www.hip-books.com

High Noon Books: www.highnoonbooks.com

Fee Required Site:

Edhelper printable leveled books:
www.edhelper.com

Notes for
Discussion Leaders

Discussion Questions

Discussion Groups

Are you interested in sharing the information in this book with other parents? Planning a *Home Grown Readers* discussion group is as easy as 1, 2, 3.

1. Read the book, including the 'Discussion Questions' and the 'Notes for Discussion Readers' (Appendix 9) Write down your thoughts, questions and comments.

2. Gather a group of interested parents and schedule a series of 60-90 minute meetings. Decide whether you will lead all discussions or share the facilitater role. I suggest a series of four to six meeting to cover all twelve chapters of the book.

3. Use the text, discussion questions and notes to guide a time of sharing about ways to help children learn to read. Be sure to provide a relaxed environment in which everyone is free to share experiences and opinions.

Author Contact Information:

Feel free to contact me with your questions, problems or reports of great reading growth. Or if you are interested in Hosting a *Home Grown Readers Workshop*.

Jan Pierce, M.Ed.
www.janpierce@comcast.net
www.janpierce.net

Appendix 9

Notes for
Group Discussions

Parents, as I said earlier, this book is for you. You want your children to read well and you're in the trenches each day working with them as they learn. You're the one who encourages them and monitors their progress. Sometimes it feels like a lonely road. Luckily you have resources. You can read books like this one to help you find the right strategies and to encourage you to set high standards for your readers.

You don't have to "go it alone."

Sometimes it helps to talk with other parents whose children are the same age. You'll find a wide diversity in reading abilities, but the basic learning issues are the same. Maybe you belong to a group of parents who regularly share their experiences of parenting young children. Maybe you home school and network with other home schoolers. Maybe you belong to the parent organization of your local school. Whatever the group, the members will benefit from going through the questions for each chapter of **Homegrown Readers**.

If you choose to read the book together, you can select a discussion leader for each meeting or decide on a permanent facilitator. If teachers use the book, they'll find these questions helpful in directing the conversation. It can be a comfortable, casual setting.

The *Notes for Discussion Leaders* will take the worry out of the process of leading the discussion because the main ideas for each chapter are simple and straightforward.

If your child has been referred for extra reading help, it's all the more important for you as the parent to be part of the process. Children with reading challenges need consistent, positive support.

Homegrown Readers and the strategies you'll find here will help you focus on specific skills and overall reading comprehension.

Remember, learning to read is a developmental process and each child has his or her internal clock setting the rate of progress. Not all children learn to read easily, but all can improve their skills with patient, positive support. The stakes are high. Learning to read opens the door to the world of learning. Let's work together to open the door wide.

Jan Pierce, M.Ed.

Appendix 9

Notes for
Discussion Leaders

If you're taking on the role of discussion leader for the *Homegrown Reader* book—good for you. To make the sessions profitable, remember to make the gathering a casual, comfortable time of sharing ideas. The goal is to help all participants understand the main ideas in each chapter.

Keep in mind that many adults don't have warm, fuzzy memories of learning to read. They may have felt embarrassed or ashamed of their progress in the learning to read process. They want their own children to learn to read without negativity. This book can help.

Here are the main ideas for each chapter. While there are some basic concepts in each chapter, there is ample room for sharing opinions and exploring varied methods of helping a child learn to read.

Key Ideas for Each Chapter

Chapter One

1. Learning to read English is a complex process.

2. English is not a highly phonetic language. Up to half of our vocabulary does not follow phonetic rules.

3. It is important to have other reading skills in place (in addition to phonics) to learn to read.

4. Some children learn to read quickly, others take more time.

5. Learning to read needs to be a positive experience.

Chapter Two

1. The home is the child's first "school." The learning environment in the home is extremely important.

2. Children should hear 500 stories before entering school.

3. Reading readiness includes a group of understandings such as left to right, top to bottom, a sense of "book language," beginning, middle and end, and much more.

4. Reading quality books ensures the reading times will be enjoyable and educational.

5. Children will have a positive attitude toward learning to read if they've enjoyed many story times.

Chapter Three

1. Reading aloud to children is the best way to prepare them to learn to read.

2. Parents need to be role models for literacy.

3. Reading aloud builds background knowledge, invites creativity and opens doors to conversations about ideas and facts--- the world of books.

4. Children know whether or not their parents enjoy books. And, children want to follow their parents' lead.

5. There are perfect books available for every age from babies to adults.

Chapter Four

1. Young children love the rhythm and rhymes of books.

2. Children find certain books to love and want to hear them over and over.

3. When a child loves a certain book, he remembers it word for word.

4. Memorization of an entire book is a good thing leading to pre-reading skills.

5. Pretend reading of a book is good practice for later reading lessons.

Chapter Five

1. Adults generally read automatically without thinking about strategies.

2. There are strategies to solve various reading problems.

3. Certain prompts help to solve a specific reading error.

4. Parents who know how to give the correct prompt will help their child solve reading problems on their own.

5. Prompts are usually short questions such as "Does that sound right?" or "Does that make sense?"

Chapter Six

1. Asking questions before, during and after reading helps a child think about the meaning of a text.

2. The goal is for adults to model asking questions and for children to learn to do it themselves as they read.

3. Reading fluently without understanding isn't real reading.

4. Reading with understanding involves noticing many "clues" along the way. These might be found in the pictures, or in key words, charts, maps, titles, etc.

5. Reading comprehension involves many skills, used simultaneously. Making sense is key.

Chapter Seven

1. Children need instruction in learning to select books at their reading level.

2. The five finger method often works in choosing a just right book.

3. The purpose for selecting a book will dictate the difficulty level. Parents may read to the child a book more difficult than they can read alone. An independent book needs to be just right. Easy books are great for practice.

4. Children must learn to know their own reading preferences.

5. It's good to help children push their boundaries and read something new part of the time.

Chapter Eight

1. Parents can learn a lot about their child's reading skills just by listening and noting the kinds of errors made.

2. Accuracy is reading each word correctly.

3. Fluency is the way a reader sounds. It is sometimes called prosody.

4. Reading rate is how fast or slow a reader says the words.

5. Reading understanding may be measured by retells or answering questions about the story.

Chapter Nine

1. A retell means naming the characters, the setting and telling the main events of the story in sequential order.

2. If a child can do a retell with a high degree of accuracy, we know he has understood the story.

3. Doing a retell takes practice. Children need to understand what is expected.

4. Parents can prompt with a question if a child misses a major event in the story.

5. Retells are great beginning points for discussion of story themes.

Chapter Ten

1. Some children become very discouraged with their progress in learning to read.

2. Older children with poor reading skills need books at their interest level, not "baby books."

3. Many boys need direction to books about adventure or non-fiction topics that interest them.

4. High interest books with lower skill levels are available, but not always on library shelves.

5. Parents can play a key role in encouraging reluctant readers by staying positive and providing the right materials.

Chapter Eleven

1. Although reading is a passive act physically, it can and should engage the mind. Imagination, creativity, drama and art flow out of the pages of a book.

2. Parents can capitalize on reading enjoyment by allowing and encouraging reading extension activities.

3. Children who struggle with the act of reading still enjoy and learn from extension activities.

4. The goal of reading extensions is deeper understanding of the text.

5. Allow children to choose the extensions they enjoy most. Art, drama, word study, etc.

Chapter Twelve

1. Sad, but true, young children lose their reading skills if they don't practice them regularly.

2. A two to three month vacation away from reading is a very long time in a child's life.

3. A summer reading program at home or through a local library or bookstore is a good way to ensure practice.

4. Reading regularly is a discipline. Some kids enjoy it more than others, but it's important to do.

5. A simple reward system makes summer reading more fun for everyone.

Appendix 9

Discussion Questions

1. Can you remember learning to read? What were the methods used? Phonics? Sight words? Did you read aloud in a small group? Other? What did you enjoy about learning to read? Does any experience stand out in your memory? Any negative experiences?

2. Why do you think the sounds of w and y are harder than other letter sounds to learn? How can we help children with tricky reading skills? Why do some children reverse letters when they write?

3. What can parents do to help when a child is fearful of the reading process? What can you do when children can't seem to remember letter names and sounds?

4. What is the value of pre-reading a book, brainstorming words, taking a picture walk or making predictions about what may happen in the book?

5. How can parents make reading time more fun? Why is it helpful to make reading an enjoyable experience?

Chapter Two: Cracking the Code: Why Learning to Read is a Complex Process

1. Do you believe reading is an essential skill? Is it more important than math or science? Why? Why not?

2. Name five ways reading aloud to children builds readiness for learning to read.

3. How does learning to read mirror learning to speak?

4. What are some ways parents can encourage a love of reading? Can you think of parental "no-no's"--- things you should not do?

5. Problem: David is four years old, has seldom listened to stories and would rather run and play than sit down to read. How would you help him get ready for learning to read in kindergarten and first grade?

Chapter Three: Bedtime Stories and More: Why It's So Important to Read Aloud to Children

1. What did you learn about reading instruction from my illustration of getting ready for a fishing trip? List three ideas.

2. What would you do if a child didn't know the meaning of words such as letter, word, line, sentence, etc.?

3. How would you respond if your child wanted to read a book that was much too hard for him? Why?

4. What do babies learn when parents read to them?

5. What is background knowledge? Why is it important in learning to read a particular book?

Chapter Four: Building Reading Skills: Why It's Okay to "Just Memorize"

1. What book does (did) your child want to hear over and over? Can you tell why she liked it so much?

2. What do we know about a child's reading development if he says three or four words while pointing to one or two?

3. In your opinion, what mistakes could parents make while helping their child read?

4. How can talking about the title of a book before reading enhance the reading experience?

5. What do we mean when we say reading is developmental? Can you think of another skill that is developmental?

Chapter Five: Strategies Good Readers Use

1. What is automaticity? In what other skills do we experience this?

2. How do you know which prompt to give when your child is "stuck."

3. What are the pluses and minuses of using flash cards for reading instruction? (Hint: it's all about meaning.)

4. Your child says store for the word story. What prompt would you use? Why?

5. Your child stops and is stuck on the word *department*. What prompt might you use? Why?

Chapter Six: Asking Questions to Improve Reading Comprehension

1. How can you tell if your child understands what she reads?

2. Name some reading behaviors that are clues to either understanding or lack of comprehension.

3. Let's say your child is reading the fairy tale, Hansel and Gretel. What are some questions you might ask before beginning the reading session?

4. What questions may arise as you read the story? (Hansel and Gretel) At the end of the story?

5. Asking questions can be tricky for children. They're not sure how to begin. Finish these prompts using Hansel and Gretel.

> • I wonder why…
> • Did Hansel and Gretel…
> • What might happen if Hansel and Gretel…
> • What would you do if…

Chapter Seven: Helping Children Choose a "Just Right" Book

1. How can you tell if a book is too difficult for your child? What are some of your child's behaviors when the book is too hard?

2. Can you think of positive ways to use books that are too hard for your child?

3. What are some book topics or genres your child loves? Why is it important to know what she loves?

4. When your child reads independently, he needs a "just right" book. What does that mean to you? How could your child use the five finger method of book selection?

5. Can you list several books that are just right for your child now? What is too easy? What would be a good book to save for adult read-alouds?

Chapter Eight: Evaluating Your Child's Reading Skills

1. Can you remember reading aloud in front of other children? How did that feel?

2. What happens when your child makes a reading error? Does he stop, skip over it? Say something else? Other?

3. What do the types of errors made tell you about your child's reading skills?

4. Explain the four kinds of reading skills listed in this chapter.

- Accuracy
- Fluency
- Rate
- Understanding

5. Which skill seems most important to you? Why?

Chapter Nine: Retelling a Story: A Great Way to Measure Comprehension

1. Name some reasons children can sound like fluent readers but not understand the meaning.

2. In the story of The Three Bears, what could you ask your child about the characters?

3. How does learning about the setting of a story help your child understand the story better? Give examples.

4. How will words like first, next, last or first, second, third help your child with retelling a story?

5. What prompt could you give when your child misses a major section when retelling a story?

Chapter Ten: Choosing High Interest Books for Reluctant Readers

1. What are your child's favorite kinds of books?

2. Why do you think children become discouraged in learning to read?

3. Name three types of reading materials that are not traditional books.

4. Think of some skill that intimidates you. Can you say why?

5. What would be the benefit to discouraged readers of finding high interest books written at a lower level of difficulty?

Chapter Eleven: Ten Easy Ways to Make Reading More Fun

1. What reading extensions do you remember doing as a child? Did you enjoy them?

2. Does your child enjoy fiction (pretend) or non-fiction (real) books more? Give an example.

3. What sorts of positive behaviors might take place as children work on a mural or chart relating to a story?

4. What would be a good reading extension for a withdrawn, shy child? How about a social, outgoing child?

5. What is your favorite story of all time? What did you enjoy about it and why? What extension would you choose to do for that story as an adult?

Chapter Twelve: Keep Them Reading Over the Summer

1. What has worked for your family in summer reading? What is a challenge?

2. What reading programs does your local library or book store offer?

3. How often do you read aloud to your children? What would make the experience more fun for you and your children?

4. Have you tried books on tape? Other types of media such as reading websites? What are their benefits?

5. What would it take to lead a children's book club in your neighborhood? Do you think kids would enjoy it? Why?

About the Author.
Notes, Comments
& Credits

About
the Author

About the Author

Jan Pierce, M. Ed.

Educator, Freelance Writer

Jan Pierce is a freelance writer living in the beautiful Pacific Northwest. She had a long and rewarding career in elementary education as a classroom teacher and reading specialist before picking up her pen (keyboard) and beginning to write.

She attended *Washington State University* and received her Master's Degree with an endorsement in reading instruction from the *University of Portland*. She has been married for 48 years to her wonderful husband, Roger, has two grown children with terrific spouses and three grandsons.

Jan has been published in a wide array of Christian and secular magazines including *Momsense* and *Young Child*. She has an essay in the parenting book, *Just Moms: Conveying Justice in an Unjust World,* published by Barclay Press. She has written for the award winning grandparenting website, *Askgranny.com* for seven years.

She regularly publishes articles on parenting and family life in regional parenting magazines

She is writing a historical novel set in 1870's India. Jan and her husband travel to India where they teach English, and support schools and orphanages. Find them at *www.onehandfulofrice.org*. Jan is an active member of *Oregon Christian Writers* and was recently nominated for the *Cascade Award* in the short article category. She is a member of *American Christian Fiction Writers* at both the national and district levels.

Jan specializes in education, parenting and family life articles and has compiled her articles on teaching children to read into this book entitled *Homegrown Readers: Simple Ways to Help Your Child Learn to Read*. Most of the information in *Homegrown Readers* first appeared in *The Mother's Heart Magazine*, owned and published by Kym Wright.

Book Ordering Information

Homegrown Readers: Simple Ways to Help Your Child Learn to Read

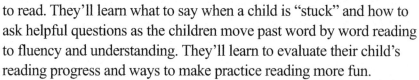

Homegrown Readers was written with parents in mind. With many years of experience teaching beginning readers, Jan has learned simple but important ways to help a child gain confidence while mastering the skills necessary to read fluently.

Parents will gain insight into the best ways to support their children as they learn to read. They'll learn what to say when a child is "stuck" and how to ask helpful questions as the children move past word by word reading to fluency and understanding. They'll learn to evaluate their child's reading progress and ways to make practice reading more fun.

Reading with understanding is a skill that opens the way for children to learn virtually anything, and ***Homegrown Readers: Simple Ways to Help Your Child Learn to Read*** can help them achieve that goal.

Order on-line or from your local book store.

ISBN 978-0-9909764-0-0   www.JanPierce.net

Notes & Credits

Credits & Thanks

Dr. Sue Stadler
Cheryl Johnson, M. Ed.
Heather Baron, M. Ed.
Kym Wright, *The Mother's Heart*
Jan Brett, Author

Please Note:

Homegrown Readers makes no claim of solving all reading problems for children with special needs or learning disabilities. However, the principles outlined in the book will help most readers make progress in reading skills.

Together we can do this!

Notes

Notes

Notes

Notes

Notes

Notes

Contacts

Contacts

CPSIA information can be obtained
at www.ICGtesting.com
Printed in the USA
LVOW13s2322070617
537351LV00029B/1084/P

9 780990 976400